Text copyright © 1990 by Random House, Inc. Illustrations copyright © 1990 by Christopher Santoro. All rights reserved under International and Pan-American Copyright Conventions. Published in the United States by Random House, Inc., New York, and simultaneously in Canada by Random House of Canada Limited, Toronto.

Library of Congress Cataloging-in-Publication Data Herman, Gail. Make way for trucks : big machines on wheels/by Gail Herman ; illustrated by Christopher Santoro. p. cm. Summary: Describes different types of trucks and the jobs they do in the city, on the farm, and at the airport, lumber mill, and construction site. ISBN 0-679-80110-3 (trade) 0-679-90110-8 (lib. bdg.) 1. Trucks — Juvenile literature. [1. Trucks.] I. Santoro, Christopher, ill. II. Title. TL230.15.H47 1990 629.224 — dc20 89-34458 AC CIP

Manufactured in the United States of America 1 2 3 4 5 6 7 8 9 10

Make Way For TRUCKS

Big Machines on Wheels

By Gail Herman

Illustrated by Christopher Santoro

Random House New York

Make way for trucks.

Tiny trucks, huge trucks.
Round trucks, square trucks.
Short trucks, long trucks.
Light trucks, heavy trucks.
Trucks do jobs.
They lift and haul.
They push, they pull.
They move people.
They move things.
Trucks deliver everything.
Uphill, downhill.
Mile after mile.
Town to town and
coast to coast.
In the city and
in the country.
On rocky, bumpy roads.
Through noisy, busy streets.
Down super-smooth highways.
In the morning,
in the evening,
and in the dark of night.
Small wheels, big wheels.
Giant wheels, monster treads.
Trucks with three wheels,
trucks with eighteen!
Mighty trucks.
Mighty wheels.
Rolling down your street right now!

Rumble-rumble-rumble. Early in the morning the garbage truck trundles through the quiet streets. Sanitation workers lift the trash and heave it into the back of the truck. A special machine presses it down. *Crunch!* There's lots more room now. Keep that garbage coming!

Look out! A fallen tree branch is blocking the road.
The cherry picker cranks its long arm up—higher and
higher still!—lifting a worker to saw the branch off.
Buzzzz! All clear!

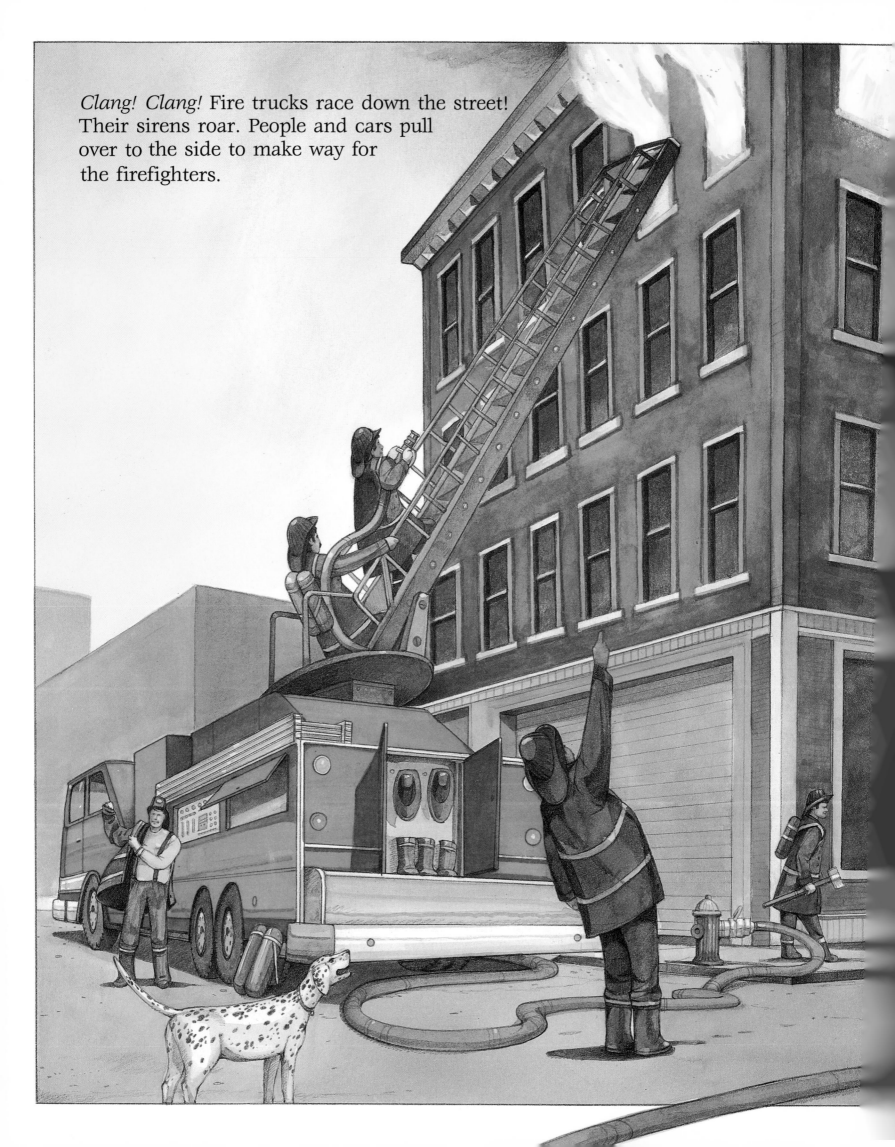

Clang! Clang! Fire trucks race down the street!
Their sirens roar. People and cars pull
over to the side to make way for
the firefighters.

There's the fire! The trucks screech to a halt. Firefighters jump off and spring into action.

The fire chief shouts his instructions. Firefighters unload the hoses from the pumper truck. The biggest hose hooks up to the fire hydrant. The hook-and-ladder truck raises its tall aerial ladder up, up to the very top floor.

Firefighters climb high, carrying their hoses. They give the signal and—*Whooosh!*—out comes the water to douse the flames.

Hooray! At last the fire is out. Thanks to the firefighters and their trucks. Time to cruise back to the fire station and scrub down these sooty trucks.

A wrecking ball smashes against the wall and topples an old building. *Boom! Crash!*

Clankety-clank. A bulldozer comes roaring through, pushing the rubble aside. Down and away with the old building, up with the new!

Look, up in the sky! A skyscraper is rising up, and trucks are helping to build it.

"We need more concrete!" shouts a worker. Here comes the mixer now. In goes the water, clay, limestone, and gravel. *Whirrr.* Round and round, the barrel spins and mixes. Out slides the heavy, wet concrete.

Going up! One crane lifts a slab of solid concrete right to the top. Another crane lifts some heavy steel girders.

Trucks are on the job, working hard from start to finish!

A scissors truck cranks its sturdy body up to the
airplane door. Workers shuttle back and forth,
carrying food and supplies from the truck right into
the airplane.

"All set for passengers now!" says a member of
the crew.

Clear the runways! There's been a snowstorm! Giant snow blowers rumble across the airstrip. *Crack!* Their huge blades chop up the hard-packed snow. *Hisss!* A gigantic fan blows the snow away.
    Ready for takeoff!

Trucks are everywhere—at fires, building sites, airports, and even at launch pads.

Slowly, slowly a crawler transporter creeps along, carrying its precious cargo—a space shuttle and its platform—to the launch pad. The biggest, and the slowest, truck in the world, the crawler transporter weighs 17 million pounds!

At last the shuttle is in place. Slowly, slowly the crawler backs out.

10, 9, 8...Blast off!

Trucks on the farm work around the clock. A pickup truck carries a load of peas, fresh from the vine.

Baa, baa! A stake truck takes sheep from one end of the farm to the other. For long distances farmers use livestock trucks. They're closed-in trucks with open-air slats on the sides so the animals can breathe.

At the dairy, farmers use special machines to milk the cows. Then they pipe the milk from the machines into gleaming tanker trucks headed for the processing plant.

This tanker truck is like a giant refrigerator on wheels. Brrr. The cold air inside keeps the milk fresh, but up front the driver is snug and warm.

Slosh, slosh goes the milk, in through a hole at the top of the tank. See how the truck and the milk machines sparkle! Dairy workers keep everything clean and shiny so the milk is as pure and healthy as can be when it gets to your table.

Timber! Loggers and their trucks are hard at work clearing a forest. One worker drives a tree crusher. *Crash!* The heavy bar in front pushes the trees down. *Splat!* Its giant wheels press down on tree stumps, flattening them like pancakes.

A log feller saws through a tree trunk with its giant blade. Its long arm holds on tight and lifts the tree right off the ground.

A grapple skidder lifts and carries the logs. *Thud! Thud! Thud!* They land smack on top of a logging truck. Now it's on to the lumber mill, where the logs will be cut into boards and used to build all sorts of things.

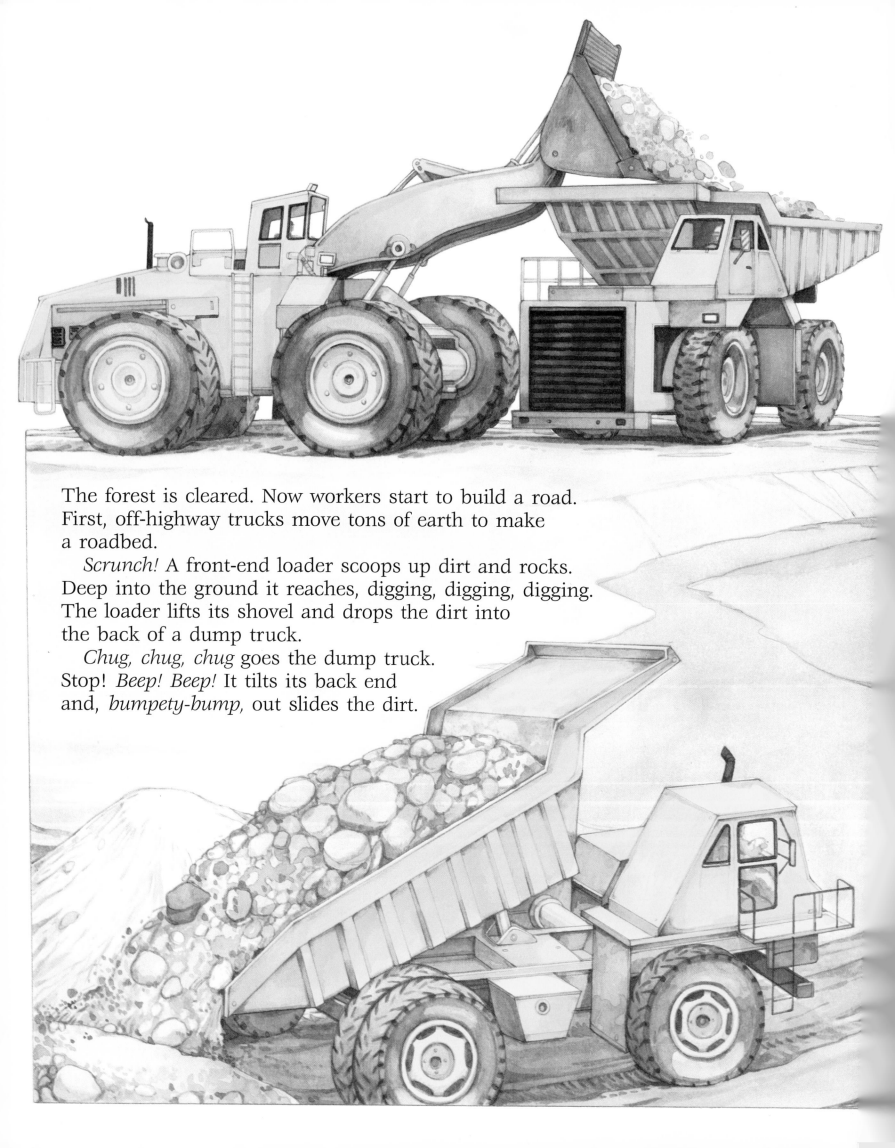

The forest is cleared. Now workers start to build a road.
First, off-highway trucks move tons of earth to make
a roadbed.

Scrunch! A front-end loader scoops up dirt and rocks.
Deep into the ground it reaches, digging, digging, digging.
The loader lifts its shovel and drops the dirt into
the back of a dump truck.

Chug, chug, chug goes the dump truck.
Stop! Beep! Beep! It tilts its back end
and, bumpety-bump, out slides the dirt.

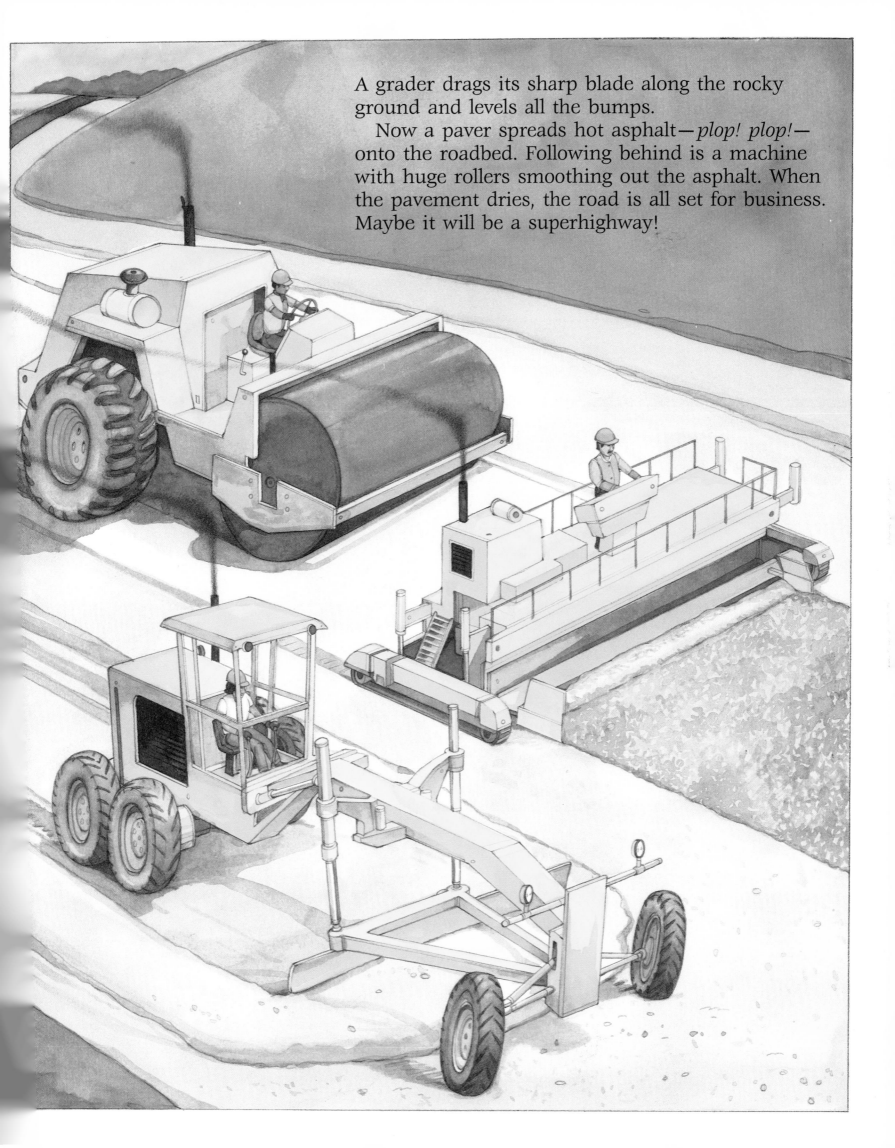

A grader drags its sharp blade along the rocky ground and levels all the bumps.

Now a paver spreads hot asphalt—*plop! plop!*—onto the roadbed. Following behind is a machine with huge rollers smoothing out the asphalt. When the pavement dries, the road is all set for business. Maybe it will be a superhighway!

Beep! Beep! Here come the tractor-trailers, tooting down
the highway. The tractor is the front part of the truck,
where the driver sits. Sometimes there's a cozy bunk bed
behind the seat—and maybe even a TV!—in case the
driver needs to rest and relax.

The trailer is the back part of the truck—the part
that trails behind! Tractor-trailers can have as many as
eighteen wheels and carry almost anything you can
imagine—even other trucks!

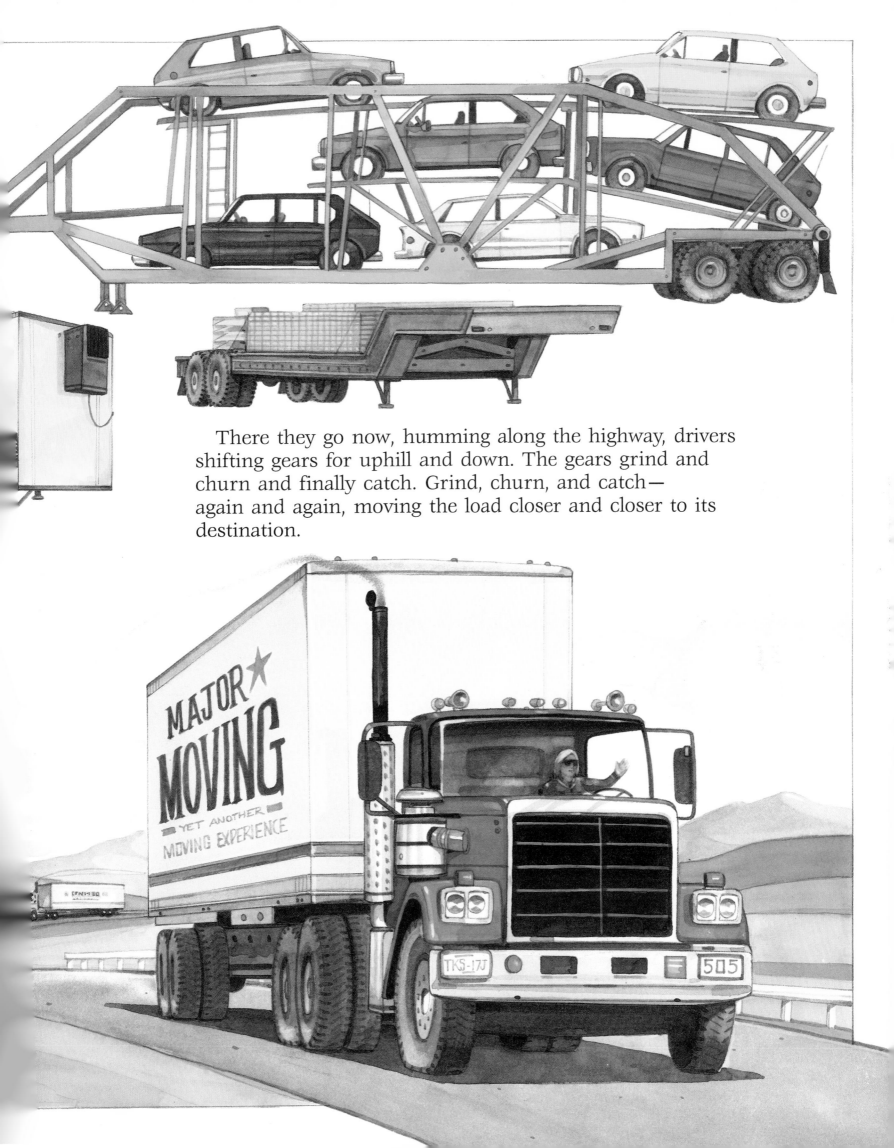

There they go now, humming along the highway, drivers shifting gears for uphill and down. The gears grind and churn and finally catch. Grind, churn, and catch— again and again, moving the load closer and closer to its destination.

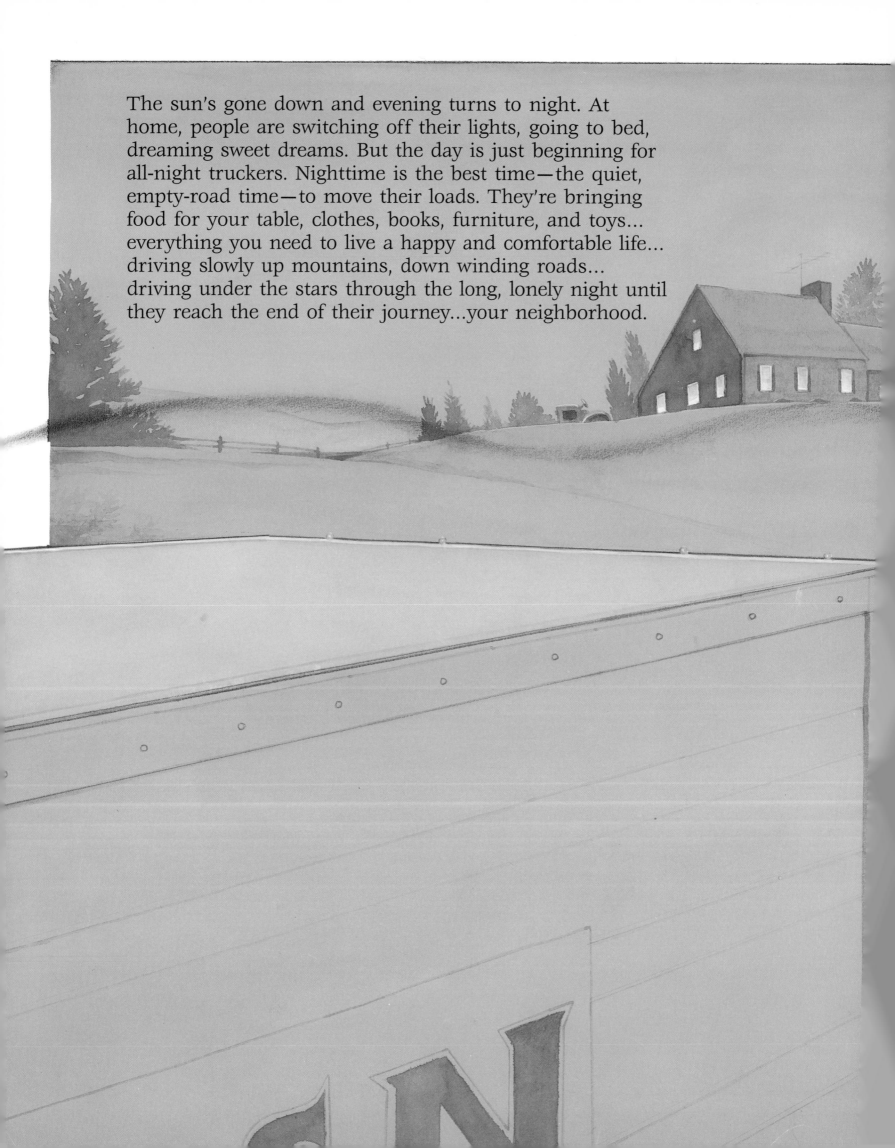

The sun's gone down and evening turns to night. At
home, people are switching off their lights, going to bed,
dreaming sweet dreams. But the day is just beginning for
all-night truckers. Nighttime is the best time—the quiet,
empty-road time—to move their loads. They're bringing
food for your table, clothes, books, furniture, and toys...
everything you need to live a happy and comfortable life...
driving slowly up mountains, down winding roads...
driving under the stars through the long, lonely night until
they reach the end of their journey...your neighborhood.